https://www.amazon.com/dp/B07Y4LM6NZ

Want to have some FUN?
Here is a brand new concept - - - there is nothing else like it anywhere!

MUSIC BASED PUZZLES!

There are 60 Sudoku puzzles (from very easy to extreme) where the numbers have all been replaced by music icons... 1/2 Notes, 1/4 notes, clefs, etc. PLUS another 60 puzzles that are mazes in music based shapes, pianos, clefs, trumpet, drum set, and on and on. Note: Most puzzle books have mazes that are aimed at kids - not these! They range from easiest to medium, to hard, to OMG!

Be sure to have an eraser, you'll need it!

Have some fun with your music passion in a brand new totally unique way! You are going to have hours and hours of fun solving these puzzles!

Order a copy for yourself and some extras for your friends - they'll like them too!

Lyrics - Class Notes - Music Ideas

Lyrics - Class Notes - Music Ideas

Lyrics - Class Notes - Music Ideas

Lyrics - Class Notes - Music Ideas

Lyrics - Class Notes - Music Ideas

Lyrics - Class Notes - Music Ideas

Lyrics - Class Notes - Music Ideas

Lyrics - Class Notes - Music Ideas

Lyrics - Class Notes - Music Ideas

Lyrics - Class Notes - Music Ideas

Lyrics - Class Notes - Music Ideas

Lyrics - Class Notes - Music Ideas

Lyrics - Class Notes - Music Ideas

Lyrics - Class Notes - Music Ideas

Lyrics - Class Notes - Music Ideas

Lyrics - Class Notes - Music Ideas

Lyrics - Class Notes - Music Ideas

Lyrics - Class Notes - Music Ideas

Lyrics - Class Notes - Music Ideas

Lyrics - Class Notes - Music Ideas

Lyrics - Class Notes - Music Ideas

Lyrics - Class Notes - Music Ideas

Lyrics - Class Notes - Music Ideas

Lyrics - Class Notes - Music Ideas

Lyrics - Class Notes - Music Ideas

Lyrics - Class Notes - Music Ideas

Lyrics - Class Notes - Music Ideas

Lyrics - Class Notes - Music Ideas

Lyrics - Class Notes - Music Ideas

Lyrics - Class Notes - Music Ideas

Lyrics - Class Notes - Music Ideas

Lyrics - Class Notes - Music Ideas

Lyrics - Class Notes - Music Ideas

Lyrics - Class Notes - Music Ideas

Lyrics - Class Notes - Music Ideas

Lyrics - Class Notes - Music Ideas

Lyrics - Class Notes - Music Ideas

Lyrics - Class Notes - Music Ideas

Lyrics - Class Notes - Music Ideas

Lyrics - Class Notes - Music Ideas

Lyrics - Class Notes - Music Ideas

Lyrics - Class Notes - Music Ideas

Lyrics - Class Notes - Music Ideas

Lyrics - Class Notes - Music Ideas

Lyrics - Class Notes - Music Ideas

Lyrics - Class Notes - Music Ideas

Lyrics - Class Notes - Music Ideas

Lyrics - Class Notes - Music Ideas

Lyrics - Class Notes - Music Ideas

Lyrics - Class Notes - Music Ideas

Lyrics - Class Notes - Music Ideas

Lyrics - Class Notes - Music Ideas

Lyrics - Class Notes - Music Ideas

Lyrics - Class Notes - Music Ideas

Lyrics - Class Notes - Music Ideas

Lyrics - Class Notes - Music Ideas

Lyrics - Class Notes - Music Ideas

Lyrics - Class Notes - Music Ideas

Lyrics - Class Notes - Music Ideas

Lyrics - Class Notes - Music Ideas

Made in the USA
Coppell, TX
08 November 2019